Pet Corner

GREAT GUINEA PIGS

By Rose Carraway

Gareth Stevens
Publishing

Please visit our website, www.garethstevens.com. For a free color catalog of all our high-quality books, call toll free 1-800-542-2595 or fax 1-877-542-2596.

Library of Congress Cataloging-in-Publication Data

Carraway, Rose.
Great guinea pigs / Rose Carraway.
     p. cm. — (Pet corner)
Includes index.
ISBN 978-1-4339-6291-2 (pbk.)
ISBN 978-1-4339-6292-9 (6-pack)
ISBN 978-1-4339-6289-9 (library binding)
1. Guinea pigs as pets—Juvenile literature. I. Title.
SF459.G9C37 2012
636.935'92—dc23

                              2011020897

First Edition

Published in 2012 by
Gareth Stevens Publishing
111 East 14th Street, Suite 349
New York, NY 10003

Copyright © 2012 Gareth Stevens Publishing

Editor: Katie Kawa
Designer: Andrea Davison-Bartolotta

Photo credits: Cover, pp. 1, 13, 15, 17, 19, 21, 23, 24 (pellets, wood) Shutterstock.com; p. 5 iStockphoto/Thinkstock; p. 7 iStockphoto.com; p. 9 Roy Mehta/Photonica/Getty Images; pp. 11, 24 (fur) Steve Teague/Dorling Kindersley/Getty Images.

Printed in the United States of America

CPSIA compliance information: Batch #CW12GS: For further information contact Gareth Stevens, New York, New York at 1-800-542-2595.

Contents

Playtime! 4

Staying Healthy 10

Furry Friends 22

Words to Know 24

Index. 24

Guinea pigs make
fun pets!

Guinea pigs hide.
This is how they play.

A guinea pig lives
in a big cage.
It needs room to run.

A person brushes its fur.
This helps it stay clean.

A guinea pig's teeth
never stop growing!

It chews wood.
This keeps
its teeth short.

Guinea pigs eat
special food.
These are called pellets.

They need to eat
two times every day.

They need to eat
fruit too.
They eat oranges.

Guinea pigs like
to live together.

23

Words to Know

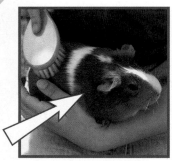
fur

pellets

wood

Index

cage 8

eat 16, 18, 20

fur 10

teeth 12, 14